G000055504

SEO Help: 20 Search Engine Optimization steps to get your website to Google's #1 page

David Amerland

Online Success Series

SEO Help: 20 Search Engine Optimization steps to get
your website to Google's #1 page

Published by Web Direct Studio, 118 Gatley Road,
Cheadle, Cheshire, SK8 4AD, UK.

This eBook is made available at:
www.webdirectstudio.com and all major online eBook
retailers including Amazon and the Sony store.

Editing, cover and interior design by WebDirectStudio
www.webdirectstudio.com (website)
info@webdirectstudio.com (email)

including this condition being imposed on the subsequent purchaser.

Limit of Liability / Disclaimer of Warranty
Whilst the author and publisher have used their best efforts in preparing this publication, they make no representations of warranties with respect to the accuracy or completeness of its contents and specifically disclaim any implied warranties of merchantability or fitness for a particular purpose. No warranty may be created or extended by sales representatives or sales materials. The advice and strategies contained herein may not be suitable for your situation. You should consult with a professional where appropriate. Neither the author nor publisher shall be liable for the use or non-use of the information contained herein. The fact that a website or organization is referred to in this publication as a citation and/or potential source of further information does not mean that the author or publisher endorses the information that the website or organization may provide or recommendations it may make.

License
Purchase of this publication entitles the buyer to keep one copy on his or her computers (when in digital format) that are for personal use and to print out one copy only. The buyer is not permitted to electronically post it, install it or distribute it in a manner that allows access by others.

The scanning, uploading and distributing of this publication via the Internet, or via any other means, without the permission of the publisher, is illegal and punishable by law. Please purchase only authorized electronic editions, and do not participate or encourage electronic piracy of copyrighted materials. Your support of the author's rights is appreciated.

For all those who know me, a big thank you for putting up with me. And for N, thank you. You just make everything else possible.

It's all about being found!

When you have a website you know that everything that it is about, its ability to function as it should and your opportunity to make money depend on a single thing: online visibility. There are three leading search engines on the web at the time of writing: Google, Yahoo! and BING. Google controls about 85% of global searches and, I know from factual experience that while having your site to the top page of all three search engines is a boost to the ego and the kind of thing that marketing people love, in reality there is only one search engine that matters when it comes to delivering targeted visitors who are most likely to be converted into customers and this is Google.

Too many times I will get clients who will ask me to optimize a website so that it appears on the top pages of all three search engines in the mistaken belief that it will triple the amount of traffic that one search engine on its own can deliver.

This is not only a fallacy but also a total waste of time and money. If your website cannot be seen on Google no top positioning in Yahoo! or BING is ever going to save you. If your website is highly visible in Google it will, in time, start to appear on both Yahoo! and BING. It will make you feel good and vindicate your belief in your own website's search engine-worthiness but if you keep a close eye on your Analytics you will see that the bulk of your visitors comes from Google and this percentage also contains most of the visitors who convert into customers.

The entire point of this book is to help you make smart choices that will accomplish three things: 1. They will save you time 2. They will save you money and 3. They will help you make money.

I have used these three criteria in every bit of advice and every example I have included here. Sometimes it has been a struggle as some particularly juicy item of information or some clever piece of knowledge has been simply too good to resist. For that I apologise, it is hard sometimes to restrain myself and my enthusiasm for the web and our digital culture comes through as a result.

If you are reading this book I suppose you are being consumed by a sense of urgency. You have a website (or an idea for one) and you need to know just what you can do to get it to the top of Google in order to make money. I know that being in business, particularly an online business, is a complex combination of desire, need and passion. The journey which has taken you to this point is a complicated one and you are now ready to create an online presence which will help you go further.

The visibility of your site is paramount to your success.

Because I have been there and because I share that sense of excitement I do not, for a moment, deviate from the factual tone I have adopted in this book. Like you I am, very much, part of the digital age. I have been immersed in the web since its inception and I abhor anything which is not straightforward in terms of doing what it promises to do.

Search engine optimization, because of the many, disparate, elements which go into it and the degree of ignorance surrounding it, plus the fact that, right now, every website owner on the planet needs its services, has become the snake oil of the 21st century.

As a practicing search engine optimizer I have been privy to client communications with other SEO firms which have made my hackles rise. In the SEO world it is all too easy to promise to do something which appears to be SEO activity. It could be to build ten links and write one article a month. It could be the promise to optimize one page and create one off-site page a week. It could be anything at all. The point is that while this passes for SEO activity it has about as much effect, usually, as a stick waved in the wind. Yet, SEO firms charge good money for it.

Real SEO firms carry out constant analysis, looking at a site's positioning, analyzing its traffic. Judging where that traffic is coming from and how visitors behave when they come on the site and then makes judgment calls which result in creating all the disparate elements of SEO which lead a site to perform better in the Google search engine index.

In this book I have tackled the issue of SEO and used 20 essential steps like you are there beside me and I am training you to replace me. I have largely dispensed with explanations and focused on the practical things you need to do in order to get results and get results fast and to this end I have employed the gimmick of a brand new website being put together and needing to get indexed fast.

The field of search engine optimization changes rapidly and is in a constant state of flux. Google changes its algorithm every month in small ways and every year, at least, in a major way and every time this happens it creates havoc amongst search engine optimizers who scramble to understand what has been changed, why and what impact it will have.

For those of us working in the search engine optimization field it's part of our job. We create sites, test them, change parameters, test again. Create more sites and generally experiment to see what works. For you, with a website to promote, it should be irrelevant. Provided you have a website which delivers real value, has original content and is updated regularly you will find that Google will do everything in its power to index it correctly and serve it high up on the organic search engine results page (commonly known as SERPs).

The entire philosophy of the search engine giant has been to "Index the world's information". They make a tremendous amount of money out of that and there will come a time in the relatively near future when SEO as it is perceived today will be an unnecessary activity.

Until that happens this book will help you get your site on Google's First page and keep it there!

David, Manchester, 2010.

I have a website!

In order to best help you with the optimization of your website I have made two assumptions here: 1. That you have a brand new website which you need to optimize fast and 2. That you know nothing about SEO.

I know that the pressures of getting a new website built and then populated with content are such that optimization comes last on the list. Sometimes this happens because it is expensive and there is not enough money left, at other times this happens because you only become aware of the need for SEO at a later stage.

Either way the fact remains that if you follow the steps outlines in the twenty chapters which follow you will get the desired result.

1. Google Analytics

Your website is your online equivalent of a shop. In order to understand what you need to do more of and what you need to change you need to have a clear understanding of the behavior of everyone who comes to your website.

For that you need to have installed tracking software which is sensitive, robust and sophisticated. Your tracking software should give you visitor numbers, visitor keywords, visitor pages, visitor origins and visitor behavior (which pages did they go to once they got on your site and where did they leave from?).

Google Analytics (GA) (www.google.com/analytics/) is a free service offered by Google that generates detailed statistics about the visitors to a website. Its main highlight is that the product is aimed at marketers as opposed to webmasters and technologists from which the industry of web analytics originally grew. It is the most widely used website statistics service, currently in use at around 40% of the 10,000 most popular websites.

GA can track visitors from all referrers, including search engines, display advertising, pay-per-click networks, email marketing and digital collateral such as links within PDF documents giving you a very precise picture of what is happening on your website in terms of visitor behavior and visitor numbers.

Integrated with AdWords, users can review online campaigns by tracking landing page quality and conversions (goals). Goals might include sales, lead generation, viewing a specific page, or downloading a particular file. These can also be monetized. By using GA, marketers can determine which ads are performing, and which are not, providing the information to optimize or cull campaigns.

GA's approach is to show high level dashboard-type data for the casual user, and more in-depth data further into the report set. Through the use of GA analysis, poor performing pages can be identified using techniques such as funnel visualization, where visitors came from (referrers), how long they stayed and their geographical position. It also provides more advanced features, including custom visitor segmentation.

Users can officially add up to 50 site profiles. Each profile generally corresponds to one website. It is limited to sites which have a traffic of fewer than 5 million pageviews per month (roughly 2 pageviews per second), unless the site is linked to an AdWords campaign. As a tool it is about as powerful as it will get and it competes comfortably, in terms of performance, with much more expensive, paid-for services.

Installing Google Analytics on your website

In order to install Google Analytics (GA) on your website you need to first register for it online so the steps you need to take are:

1. Visit http://www.google.com/analytics. Enter your Google Account email and password and click Sign In. If you don't have a Google Account, click Sign up now to create one.

2. Click Sign Up.

3. Enter your Website's URL, making sure to select either http:// or https:// from the drop-down list. Enter a nickname for this account in the Account Name field, then click Continue.

4. Enter your contact information and click Continue.

5. Read the Google Analytics Terms of Service. If you agree to these terms, select the Yes checkbox and click Create New Account to continue.

6. The Tracking Instructions page that appears contains the tracking code that you'll need to paste into each page of your site.

7. Next configure your profile - It's important to configure your profile in order to get the most out of your reports. To access your profile settings do the following: In the Website Profiles table, find the profile to edit.

8. Click Edit. The Profile Settings page appears.
9. Click Edit on the Main Website Profile Information table.
10. Default page - Setting this to the default (or index) page of your site allows Google Analytics to reconcile log entries for www.example.com and www.example.com/index.html, for example. These are in fact the same page, but are reported as two distinct pages until the Default Page setting has been configured.
11. Exclude URL Query Parameters - Does your site use dynamic session or user identifiers? You can tell Analytics to ignore these variables and not count them as unique pages. Enter any query parameters to exclude, separated with commas.

Then you'll be ready to install the Google Analytics (GA) code to your site.

Basic installation - Copy and paste the code segment into the bottom of your content, immediately before the </body> tag of each page you are planning to track. If you use a common include or template, you can enter it there.

If you have a database driven site insert the tracking code on your index.php page or equivalent (eg. default.php, index.cfm).

If you have a website which has pages with frames – (an iFrame is a web page containing frames and it will generate multiple pageviews: one for the framing page (containing either a FRAMESET or IFRAME tag within its HTML code), and one for each page shown in a frame.) Bear in mind that pageviews may be somewhat inflated. Even if a page on your site only appears as a frame for another page, it is still better to tag it with the entire tracking code. If a visitor reaches the page through a search engine or a direct link from another site and the page doesn't contain the tracking code, the referral, keyword and/or campaign information from the source will be lost.

2. Keywords

Keywords are vital when it comes to search engine optimization and the online performance of your website.

In order to be able to position your website for best online performance you need to have a very clear grasp of what the keywords at the heart of it are.

There are quite a few paid-for services you can buy online which will give you the keywords you need, you do however need to start off with some idea which means that you need to have a list of at least a handful of keywords which describe your website's field, area of business and main activity.

If you do not want to pay for a keyword research tool then point your browser at: https://adwords.google.com/select/KeywordTool and put in each of the keywords in your list. This is a free service by Google which allows you to do two things at once: First check to see how heavily contested some keywords are by checking their popularity. Second you also get ideas about additional keywords and search terms you can use.

When you have carried out your research there are two things you need to take into account: 1. That the Google Keywords tool gives you results based only on that month's searches. Depending on what you are researching you may want to take into account seasonal trends (thermal socks are more likely to be popular in winter than in summer, for example). 2. That the search term results come only from the Google database. (At the moment this is not such a significant limitation but it is something worth remembering nevertheless).

Once you have done your research (and it might be worth repeating a month later), place next to each keyword you have found a number from 1 – 10 depending upon how popular it is. Make 1 the most popular keyword in terms of searches for that month and 10 the least popular.

By the time you have finished you will probably have a list which has a few keywords with a rating of 1 and a large number of keywords which you rated between 5 and 7 and probably a sprinkling of 8 – 10 ones. You will also have, in all probability, discovered some more, new keywords and search terms which you had not thought of before.

This list is your starting point. To optimize your site you will need between 1 - 3 main keywords (which means very popular and heavily contested) and the rest should be solid 4 - 8 range ones. If you have not got many in this range use them all and take a few from the 8 - 10 value range in order to give you a starting off base for your content.

You should never start your website keyword optimization strategy with more than 20 - 30 words. Anything more and it makes it hard to see what effect your efforts are having and also what you should be focusing on next in terms of thematic linking.

Armed this way you will be able to make very educated choices when it comes to choosing your content and its focus and this is a very sound foundation to build from.

Use the Funnel Effect

When you are thinking of how you will apply the keywords you have researched in terms of your website's content having an image in mind which helps you visualize it definitely helps.

Basically the Funnel Effect took its name from the fact that it tends to use a broad range of keywords which narrow down to a main one in a keyword impression of a funnel.

It is a technique which leads to thematic linking (a clever way to say that all content on your site should be relevant to what your site does) and which should be employed on your site if:

A. You are active in a field of online commerce which has a lot of competition and in which to simply 'bludgeon' search engines with a keyword (like SEO for example) would be pointless.

B. If your budget and time are limited and you need to create the strongest possible impact with what you can invest.

How to employ the Funnel Effect on your website

In order to successfully employ the Funnel effect in your keywords what you need to do is create pages of content. Using the list which you have so carefully researched earlier decide which of the keywords which you credited with a 7 - 3 value keywords you are going to use and create two, three or more pages employing them in the text.

Link those pages to a page where you use one or two of the keywords which you credited with an 2 - 1 value. Make sure that those pages also link back to the pages which link to them in return.

It really is that simple. Simple as it may seem to be in terms of keyword strategy it is also very effective in creating what is, essentially, a mini-web of interlinked pages with related keywords each pointing to the others. This helps increase the value with which search engines view these pages and the website in which they are in and it slowly begins to gain what SEO engineers call in their parlance 'SEO juice'.

If you have to choose only one thing of all the advice in this book to employ on your website then this strategy will give you the most effective, efficient and low-cost way of promoting your site on the web.

More than one way to be clever in the use of keywords

As you would expect of course this is far from the end of the story with keywords.

Keywords can be used in a wide variety of other ways to help reinforce your website's importance in your particular field and help get it to Google's first page for particular search terms.

Let's go and see what these ways are:

1. Keyword in URL – if you have no keywords in the URL of your website and no chance of getting them in there you are missing a golden opportunity to promote your website organically. If your website is already established don't worry about it. Let's move on and see what else we can do. If, however, you are thinking of starting a new website then the best practice to adopt is to think about having a URL where the first word in it is your website's main keyword, the second is the second main keyword and so on.

2. Keyword in Title tag – use your keywords in the Title tag of your page. A Title tag is one of the meta tags on your website between 10 - 60 characters long and has no special characters. depending on the type of website you have you will have access to the meta tags either through an HTML editor (like Dreamweaver) or through the Content Management System control panel through which you run your website. Keywords in the Title tag are important but if you are really

stuck here and do not know how to access the
Title Tags and have no way of doing so then
don't worry about it. Put it on your 'To Do' list
for paid-help changes which you can do at a
later date and let's move to the next one.

3. Keyword in Description meta tag –
this shows that your content is now
thematically linked and so are your keywords.
The description meta tag, unlike the Title Tag,
is easy to find in the Content Management
System control panel of your website (if your
website is dynamic) and it is also easy to find in
HTMl editors such as Dreamweaver. Best
practice says you should make the description
less than 200 characters long. Google no longer
"relies" upon this tag, but will often use it.

4. Keyword in Keyword meta tag – this
again is part of the thematic linking strategy of
your website. Every single word you use in this
tag has to also appear in the body text of your
page somewhere. If it does not you will be
penalized for spamming and irrelevance. For
best practice use fewer than 15 words to
describe each page of your website.

5. Keyword density in the body text of
your page – achieve a 1 - 3% - (all keywords/
total words) in your topic on any page on your
website. Some report topic sensitivity on this
which means that the keyword spamming
threshold varies with the topic. Best practice:
To be on the safe side keep well within the 5%
limit. If you need to calculate the keyword
density of content you are creating then check

the keyword density of your text before you drop it in by using: http://www.articleannouncer.com/tools/keyword .html to check your copy. Article Announcer is an online SEO tool that allows you to check the keyword density of the content you have created and are about to include in your site for up to three specific keywords. This way you can make sure that the content you generate for your site has a specific keyword density. It is best practice to work with one primary and two secondary keywords in each block of text you include on your website.

6. Individual keyword density – when it comes to individual keywords in your web page as a whole it is best to keep them between 1% - 3% of the total number of words used. Best practice: check your web page's keyword density with: http://www.keyworddensity.com/.

7. Keyword in H1, H2 and H3 headings – Use bold text and relevant keywords in your H1, H2 and H3 headings on your page. Header tags are essentially a way of telling search engines and human visitors which are the headings and what they are about. For best practice choose your headings carefully to appeal equally to both human readers and search engine bots.

8. Choose your keyword font size – Google treats "Strong the same as bold, italic is treated the same as emphasis". For best practice find ways to use bold text and italics on your web page without making it look like somebody's school homework.

**9.   Keyword   proximity   (for   2+
keywords)** – This is the part where you write
keywords together, for instance, on a 'Cowboy
Hat' site where you have the word 'Stetson' as
part of your keyword list you can put together a
sentence which contains both 'Cowboy Hats'
and 'Stetson'. The closer these are together in
that sentence the better it works for your
website in terms of keyword content. For best
practice place your keywords directly adjacent,
this is best as it has the greatest effect in term
of SEO.

10. Keyword phrase order – This is a
really obvious and yet often made mistake. In
the drive to include keywords in the text way
too often website owners forget to include
phrases that exactly match the query likely
searchers will make. In terms of an
SEO website, for instance a search term such as
'SEO help for my website' should be used. For
best practice: Make sure you include at least
one exact phrase in terms of the search query
those who will look for the information you
provide, will make. If I was optimizing a
website to sell cowboy hats I would definitely
include a search term such as 'Cowboy Hat to
wear on the Range' as a likely search term to be
used by some of those looking to buy Cowboy
Hats. In your keyword research there would be
a few search phrases which come up. Pick at
least one of them to reinforce in your content.

11. Keyword prominence – When it
comes to keyword placing positioning is every

bit as important as repetition, thematic linking and content relevance. This means that where your keywords appear on the text on your page is important to the importance search engines give them. Make them bold and place them near the top and you immediately increase the weighting search engines give your web page for those keywords. For best practice think carefully about where on the page you will place your keywords and try to find a way to give them prominence naturally.

12. Keywords in links and alt text – Search engines are blind. They cannot see pictures and they can follow links but not read them. Alt Text is used to describe the images you place on your site so that they are visible to search engines. Make sure that the keywords you use to describe alt text and links on your web page is complementary to the content on the page and thematically linked so that they play that all-important supportive role that's needed to convince a search engine bot of your website's importance in terms of the content and subject you are promoting. For best practice use descriptive keywords that enhance existing content. Do not spam the search engines by unnecessarily repeating keywords in alt tags you will only get your site penalized.

3. Creating Content

The reason we looked at how to research keywords is because they are the engine which drives your online content. A site without regularly changing content is a site which suffers from search engine neglect.

The thing is you did not start an online business in order to become a writer. If writing content does not come easy to you then you will find it becomes a drain on the time you have available to deal with all the other aspects of your online business.

This is where this chapter comes into its own. The aim is to provide you with ideas on how to create content quickly and efficiently.

Content Writing Plan

Arm yourself with pen and paper (or use the Notepad feature on your computer). Make a list of your website's main keywords you researched which describe the product or service it is selling. Then think up to 300 keywords in addition to the website's central ones, make sure they are all related. This is like one of those association games you used to play when you were still at school.

If you need help thinking up keywords which are peripheral to your website but still relevant use the free online keyword suggestion tool: http://freekeywords.wordtracker.com or use the free Google Keyword tool we looked at in detail in chapter 2 of this book: https://adwords.google.com/select/KeywordTool. This will also give you an idea of the popularity in searches of some of the keywords so you will be able to decide on that basis which ones to include in your list and which ones to leave out. Bear in mind that if you use the wordtracker keyword tool the results come only from overture (which means they represent only a single point of view as opposed to a global picture of search) and there is really no such thing as leaving your website's SEO to run on autopilot. You need to constantly prune, fine-tune and assess your wordlist.

For better accuracy it is worth running both the Google and Wordtracker tools and comparing the results for the main keywords. Provided you followed the instruction in chapter 2 you should have, already, a very detailed keyword list anyway.

Keyword relevancy, a two-minute guide to getting your website content completely right

Keywords in the content of your website play such a vital role that you should leave nothing to chance. Keywords are the important part of your writing. But you shouldn't have to spend

hours and hours on this, so here's what you do
with my two-minute guide:

**1. Use a two or three word
combination** that best describes your site, its
products or service, as your main keywords.
Research shows that 31% of those who carry
out an online search use two-word phrases in
the search engine field. A further quarter of all
those who use search type a three-word
combination. Just 19% of users pin their luck
on a single word. Put together sentences and
paragraphs which are descriptive and come
easy to you.

2. Choose which keywords you will use
carefully and, if possible, go for a niche within
your industry. If your site is new, going toe-to-
toe with the big, established boys will only be
disheartening. Which means if you just
appeared on the net and you sell air tickets you
shouldn't be too ambitions and target keywords
like "air tickets", instead use a combination of
peripheral words so you start showing on the
search results fast. These can be:

cheap air tickets
air tickets
air line tickets
cheap international air tickets
cheap air line tickets
travel air tickets
air tickets to....[put in here a specific
destination you specialize in]

All of these are suggestions I have just
plucked out of midair without any research.

You should go and use the Wordtracker and the Google keyword tools we looked at just above because it will give you a basis for your keyword list that is based on actual searches rather than guesses.

3. Be careful and don't get carried away and use only keywords which are so specialized that no one but an expert would use in a search engine search box. If your site sells products or services which have a technical name you will need to think of what your non-expert customers will be looking for and write copy which deliberately includes those words.

4. At the same time don't use irrelevant keywords which are not strongly reflected by your site's content, because you will start raising search engine red flags about sites that are not really what they say they are. So do not, for example, talk about kittens if you are selling cowboy hats!

5. Don't use keywords in a way which may get you banned by the search engines. Here's the kind of keyword misuse which will have exactly the opposite effect of what you want: *Cowboy hats are great because everyone who wants a Cowboy Hat should come to our Cowboy Hats website to buy a Cowboy Hat. Cowboy Hats have the best price for Cowboy Hats.* This, rather crass example, is called keyword staffing and Google has issued specific guidelines pointing out that websites that do that can get totally dropped from the Google Index. So, strong as the temptation might be to get some high keyword density in there —— do not do it!

6. Do not use images with filenames or ALT tags that may get your site filtered or banned from search engines. Note: (Alt tags are the attribute of the image that describes what the image is when the picture does not show in a web browser. Search engine bots are picture blind. They can read text but not images. This is why Alt Tags are so important. They fill in the 'missing bits' of your site allowing a search engine bot to make a value judgment on the combination of words and pictures you have created.

7. Avoid duplicating pages on your website. Duplicating pages used to be a favorite technique of webmasters looking to bulk up the content of their site. They would have largely similar content in two or three pages and search engines would place their site high thinking that it was a large site with much valuable information. Now that simply gets your site penalized so make sure you do not do it.

8. Make sure you optimize each single page you create for a set of keywords and then repeat the cycle with new content. To do this effectively you need to think in chunks of 300 words that contain your chosen keywords in the natural flow of writing.

9. Organize your new content structure so you do not bury old pages with new ones. Far too often websites have a linear structure which means that new pages which should be adding weight and credibility to your website in terms of keywords are pushed further to the back (it takes quite a few clicks to find them). When this happens it becomes obvious to search engines that they are no longer so relevant so they also discount them and with them they discount all your hard work. Try to structure your website so that it takes a maximum of two clicks to get from any page to any other page. This may well mean that you need to create archives for your content which 'open' the site up to visitors as well as to search engine bots.

10. Do not post half-finished or under-construction sites. Any page that is under-construction or is half-finished is discounted by search engines as well as human visitors. Neither will come back and check again any time soon and you will have lost your best chance to make a good impression.

How to generate content fast

Now that you know all this the question may still remain: If you really hate writing what do you do in order to write relevant content for your website?

Starting with your keywords do the following:

1. Create paragraphs which describe your website's purpose.

2. Create paragraphs which describe what you want your website to do.
3. Create paragraphs which describe why your website is unique.

You do not need to be a writer to do all this. Adopt a conversational, matter-of-fact tone, just like you would if you talked to someone in person and simply put all this in.

Then:

1. Separate your paragraphs into content which will go into different site pages.
2. Separate some of the content into thoughts and ideas which will go into a blog section of your site. Note that blogs are like diaries. They do not need to have content put in them with the structured approach of real articles and can give you an easy means of generating keyword-rich content for your site.
3. Put down some one-line title ideas which you can use to generate content. Some easy examples are: Ten reasons why you should use this website. Three things which make this website better than any competitor, etc.

While this may sound formulaic it is also a valid means of getting round the obstacle of writing content for your website.

At some point you may well be able to outsource this activity in which case the fact that you did it in the first place will allow you to guide those who will write for you in a much more constructive way.

4. Search engine submission

Search engine submission is a vital element of optimization of your site which should never be ignored. Submitting your website to the top 40 search engines for indexing is literally a case of spending a few minutes typing and then clicking 'Submit'. I know it sounds easy and I also know from experience that many a new website owner has either paid good money for the service as a one-off or paid good money for the service as a regular thing. It is hard to say that they have been 'ripped-off' by SEOs who simply saw an opportunity to make good money and seized it because what makes it so 'easy' to submit a site is knowledge which the search engine optimizers in question have paid for with hundreds if not thousands of hours of online research.

The nature of a service as opposed to a product is that you pay for the knowledge and skill inherent in an action, rather than the action itself. Yes, some website owners have paid a lot of money for something which takes a couple of minutes. The bright side to all this is that in a moment you will also know how to do this so you never have to part with another dime when it comes to submitting your site to search engines for indexing.

To submit your site for indexing simply go to the following submission services web address: http://www.localsubmit.com/free.asp. Choose 'Free Submission' from the 'Free Services' tab on the left hand side of the web page. Input your webiste address in the filed on the new page you are taken to and your email address and click 'Submit'.

There are a couple of things you need to do first:

1. Have a webmail address which you use only for the submission process. Search Engine Submission services sell the email lists they acquire to spammers (still) so this is to make sure your inbox does not get flooded with unwanted offers of services.

2. Make sure that you submit only the homepage of your site.

An often-asked question is how often should you submit your website for indexing to the major search engines?

The answer is not as simple as you may think. Go over a certain number of times and your new site gets flagged up as a spam site and quite likely get penalized for search engine index spamming. Get it wrong and you miss the opportunity to have your site's content indexed properly when you most need it.

In an ideal world a search engine bot does a complete crawl of your site each and every time it visits it. The huge size of the web and the programming complexity of websites often mean that this does not happen. If you want your site to be indexed completely each time it's visited by a search engine bot you need to make sure search engines know they should do it.

The length of time it will take for your site to be crawled is different from one search engine to another. Google will crawl your site within two weeks at the most, Yahoo! within three and most other search engines within four to six or even longer, depending on the number of websites which are submitted for indexing in their database at that particular time.

The moment you have your website submitted for indexing by the top 40 search engines of the web you have completed the first step towards crawling by a search engine. This process will get it indexed, eventually, but it is not fast.

If you have spent considerable time and money in the creation of your website each day without traffic costs you money, you understand of course that scheduled indexing takes time but there are sometimes specific reasons why you may want a particular page on a website indexed fast. There may be a time-sensitive offer, you may have a promotion or there may be another reason. The thing is that when speed counts and you really need a particular page (or two) of your site to be indexed you can no longer afford to submit it through the usual channels and then sit back and wait.

The next chapter tells you how to avoid waiting.

5. Get your website indexed fast

When you have a website nothing destroys your confidence more than not seeing it come up on searches in Google and the other search engines. All the hard work you have put in creating the content and supervising the look seems to have been for nothing. The same is also true when you have made major changes to a website and you expect to see it appear in its new format in Google's search pages and you are stuck in a waiting game.

This step is all about short-circuiting the search engine submission process and getting a site indexed fast or (as is more the case) getting a specific page of a website indexed fast.

To achieve this we will use a process called social tagging. Social tagging sites are sites which get content that is submitted by their members and is then promoted or dumped in a kind of online democracy through a voting system that the members apply. One example of a social tagging site is www.digg.com.

In addition, the social tagging networks themselves will give your site traffic which will further start driving its SEO status in the search engines' eyes and, let's face it, provide you with a certain number of new customers which, in itself, is not a bad thing.

40 social tagging sites to try

Here is a list of 40 social tagging sites for you to
use:

www.propeller.com

www.slashdot.org

www.digg.com

www.technorati.com

www.del.icio.us

www.stumbleupon.com

www.twitter.com

www.reddit.com

www.tagza.com

www.fark.com

www.newsvine.com

www.furl.net

www.swik.net

www.sphinn.com

www.blinklist.com

www.faves.com

www.blinklist.com

www.mrwong.com

www.spurl.net

www.netvouz.com

www.diigo.com

www.backflip.com

www.bibsonomy.org

www.folkd.com

www.linkagogo.com

www.indianpad.com

www.plugim.com

www.buddymarks.com

www.mylinkvault.com

www.google.com/bookmarks.com

www.jumptags.com
www.smallbusinessbrief.com/index.php
www.oyax.com
http://www.a1-webmarks.com/
www.bookmarktracker.com/bt/home
www.myvmarks.com/index.cfm
www.mixx.com/
www.wirefan.com
www.danogo.com
www.linksmarker.com
www.ximmy.com

The best way to tackle this is to open a Word file and create a three-column table. On the far left hand side place each of these and in the following columns put in the user name and password you use to register on each site. Having done that you can then click from the table each time and social tag the pages you need to have indexed fast.

6. Search Engine check

If you are serious about helping your website perform well you need to understand just how a search engine bot sees it.

Unlike people, search engine bots see the code of a website and ignore the graphics and layout which you use to guide the human visitor's eye.

This means that your carefully worked-on design and layout may actually work against you if it has an insufficient number of links on the home page linking to the site content or has poor keyword density or even insufficient content on the home page.

So, once you are ready with your links, design and content and want to see how your website looks when it is crawled by one of the search engine bots point your browser over to: http://www.seobench.com/search-engine-crawler-simulator/ and see it through the eyes of a search engine bot.

Stripped of its dressing your website should still work.

Check to see that the following apply:

1. **Content** – you have keyword-rich and theme-related content on the homepage of your website.

2. **Links** – make sure that you have a good number of links going from the home page to other pages. This is important as it allows the search engine bot to then follow these links and index all the other pages of your website.

3. **Alt text** – graphics which are invisible to search engines should still be 'visible' in terms of their description and those descriptions should complement and reinforce the theme and keywords of your website.

4. **It still works** – even though it has been stripped of nice layouts and great graphics your home page should still work in terms of identifying to the viewer what it does and how it does it.

If any of these do not work completely when you view your site this way then you need to take steps to address it.

7. Inbound linking strategy

If you want your website to perform well in terms of search engine assessment then you need to have a carefully worked out linking strategy and a detailed analysis of incoming links to your website.

This may seem obvious but these two things are totally separate and we need to look at each in turn.

Check on your website's inbound links

The number of inbound links coming into your website is important because it helps do several things at once:

1. Drive traffic to your website.
2. Drive search engine attention to your website – it is, in fact, one element of search engine marketing (SEM).
3. Elevate the importance of your website in both search engine and visitors' eyes.

Inbound links are also part of both the PageRank and TrustRank system.

PageRank is a link analysis algorithm, named after one of the Google founders, Larry Page, used by the Google search engine. The algorithm assigns a numerical weighting to each element of a hyperlinked set of documents, such as the World Wide Web, with the purpose of "measuring" its relative importance within the set. The algorithm may be applied to any collection of entities with reciprocal quotations and references. The numerical weight that it assigns to any given element is called PageRank.

Just for information purposes it's worth noting that the name "PageRank" is a trademark of Google, and the PageRank process has been patented (U.S. Patent 6,285,999). However, the patent is assigned to Stanford University and not to Google. Google has exclusive license rights on the patent from Stanford University.

If you want to check the PageRank of your website go to: http://www.prchecker.info/check_page_rank.php. Input your website's URL there and check it.

If your site has a PageRank (PR) above 1 you might also consider displaying it for visitors to see. It helps to instill confidence in those of your online visitors who are aware of the importance of PageRank.

The PageRank of a website updates on the Google database once every six months or so and the search engine takes into account elements such as inbound links (and the vicinity they come from), traffic and search

Page 43

term popularity amongst others. Google's algorithm is quite complex and the PR is split into two formats, one public (which Google makes available to the world) and one private (which it uses in its search engine algorithm).

While we can never really know how the private part of the PR algorithm works things out it is safe to assume that it is not far removed from the public one (to have a huge disparity between the two would serve no real logical purpose).

If you want to know how many other pages in different search engine databases link to your website then go to: http://www.submitexpress.com/linkpop/, input your website's URL and see exactly what has been indexed.

How do you get more links?

The real question, of course, after you have done all this is just how do you get more links?

This is where your linking strategy comes into its own. Obviously you need to have one and it needs to be consistent and consistently applied.

In order to get more links you need to have:
1. Original content which offers real value to online visitors.
2. A means for online visitors to link to your site (perhaps through

permacode or a 'Link to this page' button).

3. A means of publicizing content you create beyond the normal search engine route (and about that we will talk in detail shortly).

Provided you put these in place and cultivate your PageRank and work on your link strategy there is no reason why your site will not appear to be an important one as far as search engines are concerned.

How do you create the perfect link to your site?

1. Use the keyword in the anchor text. This is an obvious one but seven times out of ten webmasters forget to implement it (or they can't because the site they are getting a link from imposes conditions or has limitations). If your website name is, for instance, 'Bestshoesintown.com' make sure you get a descriptive anchor text from the link, which in this case would be: 'The Best Shoes in Town'.

2. Make sure the page you place the link in is relevant to your site's content. Again an obvious thing to look out for and in the excitement of actually having a link many webmasters forget to make sure that this is the case. If your website is about shoes, for instance, like in our previous example, it would help to have a link pointing to you from a page that actually talks about shoes rather than one that talks about, let's say, boats. Now, if this is not the case and there is nothing you can do to change it, irrelevance will not hurt your site's SEO but it will degrade the importance of the link you are getting a little because Google will see that it is either a paid-for link or a favor link.

3. The link's destination is also important. This is a point many webmasters miss entirely. Picture this. You're optimizing your website to sell shoes. Your link has been optimized with that in mind but it's pointing to a page on your site where you actually talk about market conditions, or your favorite walking holiday, or the need for seasonal stock levels. Anything, in short, apart from shoes. If that happens you have just lost a good opportunity to have a top-notch link giving your site some serious SEO juice.

4. The originating site's PageRank is every bit as important as all the other points discussed above. Sites which have a high PageRank give you more SEO juice than say one with a lower PageRank which means their link carries more weight. What few webmasters really know is that the Google algorithm's calculation of a site's PageRank has little to do with what the Google Toolbar tells you it is (though, in theory, it should not be far from it), which means a site with PageRank 3 giving you a link might actually be just PageRank 2 which means it's not worth all that much after all. So, if you are going to all this trouble of creating the perfect inbound link to your site you may as well do it for a site with a PageRank of at least 6.

5. The link must not have a 'No Follow' attribute. A 'No Follow' attribute stops search engine bots from following the link which means it will not lead them to your site so it may as well not be there. There are many reasons why a 'No Follow' attribute might be placed on a link by a webmaster. Maybe they are selling links and do not want Google to penalize them. Maybe they want to keep search engine bots on their site for as long as possible so they can do a deep crawl. Maybe they are involved in link fraud. Whatever the reason, bottom line is that the only way to check this is by looking at the source code of the page where the link to your site is actually based.

Just go on that page, go to the 'View Source Code' option of your web browser and then just copy and paste this into a Word file and study it to see if the 'No Follow' attribute is linked to the link leading to your website.

8. Outbound linking strategy

The conventional wisdom (if you bother to trawl SEO forums at all) is that every link that leaves your website weakens your PageRank (PR) while every link which comes into your website strengthens your PageRank (PR).

Ok, once and for the record: This is total nonsense and it has been total nonsense since Google re-worked their PageRank algorithm in 2007.

Outbound links from your site show that you have an active presence on the web which is organic and value-laden. Google sees them as a positive thing and they should be encouraged with a few provisos.

First they should be relevant to the content and theme of your website.

Second they should be used with a consistent strategy which aims at enriching your content's depth and visitor experience.

Third they should never open on a page of your site so that by clicking on any link the visitor is taken away from your site. They should always open in a new window.

Something else worth paying attention to is where links appear on your page. If you want to be sure to pass along as much PR as possible to a certain link, you should make sure that link is not in a long list of links with no other text between them. Search engines see long lists of nothing but links as being a bit spammy, so they tend to weigh these links with less importance. A link that is inside a paragraph of text is typically given more weight, because it looks like a more natural link. It looks like a news site citing a reference, or a writer linking to a particular resource.

9. Two SEO Mistakes that may be killing your site

The battle to get your site noticed is fought simultaneously on two fronts. One is your site visitors. Naturally enough you want to impress them with your site's quality, you want them to feel they are dealing with a professional website and you want them to trust it, trust you, and go away and talk about it positively with their friends and colleagues. More than that, you want them to make a purchase, buy a product or access a service.

The other is search engines bots which are, to all intents and purposes, about as susceptible to the artistic integrity of your site as your next door neighbor's dog's rubber toy.

This means that all the flashy, clever javascript and Flash button navigation you have so artistically, and probably expensively, employed is actually a stumbling block when it comes to getting all your pages indexed.

This is because search engine crawlers, clever as they might be, cannot actually read Flash and javascript so they cannot follow the links your site has to other pages. In plain English parlance it is akin to ringfencing specific pages of your site from search engine spiders and not allowing them to access the content.

Most of the navigation aids created using javascript applets and Macromedia Flash can be replicated using XHTML and CSS. Where cost and time are an issue the clever work around is to have plain text links at the bottom of your page as an additional navigation aid. These then allow the spiders to index the rest of your site, after they come to the home page, by following these links.

A similar charge is placed against the overuse of site graphics and Flash animation. Used judiciously it helps bring a site to life but it has to be done in a way that still balances a site's need to be thoroughly indexed and placed highly on organic search findings.

The use of javascript and Flash and the overuse of graphics are two common SEO mistakes even advanced site designers make. This is why an SEO audit at the end of a site's design helps pick up and fix possible SEO issues like this.

10. Check on your competitors

Working on the details of your website's SEO it is all too easy to forget that all your efforts and all your skill and all the knowledge you gather here are only as good as your competitors' SEO efforts and SEO skills and websites permit.

This should not be as shocking as it sounds. Yes, you know exactly what you need to do in order to optimize your website for fast indexing, in-depth indexing and high serving on the search engine results page but (and it a really big BUT) if your competitors' websites are older than yours, have a higher PageRank than your site and have already built up traffic for those relevant search terms, knocking them off is going to be a pretty tall order. Luckily it is not impossible. Here is what you need to do:

Understand what your competitors are doing

First of all you need to realize that in order for your site to appear higher than your competitors' sites for similar search terms you don't just need to emulate them. You need to clearly understand what they are doing and then do it better than them.

This will be possible in things you can control such as content optimization, meta tags and links (and I hope you have been through the previous chapters covering all the essential SEO techniques you need to employ), but it will also include things which you cannot control such as the age of a website, the age of the one-way links coming to it, the quality of the one-way links coming to it, the number of pages indexed and the number of quality links indexed by each search engine.

Here we will see how we can analyze each aspect in order to reach the correct conclusion. I will also stress that each analysis we run has a built-in error factor and imprecision so it will not be as conclusive as we like (and I will give an example in a moment) so it is important to tackle them all in order to build up as comprehensive a picture as possible. In terms of the imprecisions we will encounter here is an example: We will use the Internet Archive to check the age of a site by seeing when it was first spidered. The thing is that that is only an indicator. If the site has been redesigned then Google will have indexed it anew and will be out of synch in terms of how old it sees the site in its database to what the Internet Archive will report. I mention this here because it is important to understand not just the power of the tools we use for analysis but also their limitations.

1. **Make a list of your main competitors.** You may already have some idea who they are. If not use the top three-four keywords in your industry and see which ten sites consistently rank on Google's first page for them. Draw up a list and that will be your target for analysis. You will need to have a column for each of the ten sites and also include your own here as it will help you to see how you really measure up.

2. **Check a site's Age.** Let's begin by going to the following URL: http://www.archive.org/index.php. In the search field there type in turn each of your competitors' websites. Make a note of when they were first indexed. The number of pages that have been indexed is also important as it indicates importance of the site in terms of the traffic it attracts. There is little you can do to improve your site's age except focus on your own SEO activity and search engine marketing and wait.

3. **Check a competing site's back links.** One way links and how these are indexed by search engines are an important indicator of the site's PageRank in that particular search engine's index. Each search engine has a different way of indexing back links and there is a different way of querying

them. Here's how to query each search engine's index and see how many one way back links each of your competitors has. Again check your site either first or last to give you an idea:

Google: link:http://www.domainname.com
Yahoo!: linkdomain:domainname.com
BING: link:domainname.com   [Warning: BING have, for now, blocked the back link query check from their database – so it may not be possible to do it unless they bring it back]

Action Plan: If your site does not yet have many back links you will need to engage in an active campaign to build some. Make sure that at last a few of them point to pages other than the homepage. This is called Deep Linking and it helps increase the PageRank of subpages on a website.

Check the number of pages each site has indexed

The number of pages indexed by each search engine plays a vital role in the search results that each search engine will return on search queries relating to your site's content. If a search engine, for instance, has indexed just a handful of hundreds of pages on your site then it will not be able to fully serve your content for relevant search terms.

Here's how you check each of the major
search engines:

Google: site:http://www.domainname.com
Yahoo!: site:www.domainname.com
BING: site:www.domainname.com

Action Plan: If your website has not yet
been indexed deeply by any (or all) of the major
search engines you should 1. Prepare a site
map (more about that in the next chapter) 2.
Create a few Deep Links 3. Use Google Pages
pages.google.com, MSN Spaces spaces.live.com,
and Yahoo Blogs (sign up at the Yahoo.com
portal), to create pages that link back to your
site and force each search engine to follow the
links and index your site deeper and more
extensively.

Check PageRank

PageRank is something you can do little about.
It is a combination of the site's age, how
frequently it is being updated, what traffic it
gets and how many links it gets and what
quality they each have.

Here's how you check: Go to
http://www.digpagerank.com/ and input
www.domainname.com and check each of the
45 datacenters that come up there. You may
also want to think of employing the Google
Toolbar toolbar.google.com it is free, it allows

you to check every website you visit and having it while visiting your own website can have a beneficial impact in its Google standing (though a small one it must be said) as Google uses the Toolbar information it receives to check which sites are being visited when and update trends in its database.

Check Meta Tags

Have you ever considered what keywords or phrases a competitor is targeting on their website? Have a peak at their meta tags by simply viewing the webpage source. Load their page in your browser and simply View>Source. Pay particular attention to the header tags that include title, description, and keywords. Are these keywords part of your marketing mix?

11. Create the perfect Press Release to market your website online

The moment you have a website you are under pressure to market it and a Press Release has always been the traditional way of making sure that those most interested in finding out about your online business or services actually did so.

The fact is that writing a Press Release is a skillful task and a well-written Press Release that will help you market your website, costs money. Unless, of course, you take advantage of my online marketing expertise and use the Press Release template I have created for you below to actually create a powerful, professional Press Release for your website that will help you be noticed.

Here we go. Change the information in square brackets with your own:

FOR IMMEDIATE RELEASE: [Insert Date here]

[Write an eye-catching compelling headline here]
[Write your website's URL here]

[Insert here your city, state abbreviation] – Write your opening paragraph in this space. It should include your website or business name, mention of the your service, and any information about your services that you'd like to include. Make sure to include the benefits of choosing you as an expert, highlighting what about your service is unique.]

[Don`t forget to include quotes from your satisfied clients taken directly from your past-client reviews. If your text goes beyond this point, it is best to break the body of the press release up into two different paragraphs.]

[Next write something that contextualizes your service and company. Give some useful stats about your industry or line of business. Include some factual information editors can use in an article about you. Even though you are describing your expert services, remember to write the text in third-person perspective, as if it was written by someone other than yourself.]

[End your Press Release with a strong statement or quote that catches the reader's attention. The stronger the better.]

[When you are done writing, insert these three symbols at the bottom of your text - they indicate that the press release is finished.]

# # #

[In this space have your contact details, website address, contact telephone number and email and a third person statement outlining your business or your website's presence] Eg: HelpMySEO was founded in 2007 by two SEO industry experts who were determined to share their expertise in search engine optimization with the many webmasters struggling to cost-effectively optimize their websites.

After you're done writing your release, submit it to PRWeb.com, a great resource that sends your document to thousands of newspaper, magazine, radio, TV, and similar media managers. If you are also looking for some free PR coverage try any of the sites found at: http://mashable.com/2007/10/20/press-releases/

Summary

A professionally written Press Release should be a standard part of your online search engine marketing arsenal. The information above allows you to create one almost effortlessly.

Action Plan

Go through the information above and carefully substitute your own ending up with a professional-looking Press Release.

12. Six reasons why your site may drop in rank (and what to do about it)

When you are a webmaster (or even a website owner who likes to get his hands 'dirty' from time to time) a large amount of your time is spent search engine optimizing your website through the creation of new content, streamlining its architecture and cross-linking files and articles in order to increase exposure, get deeper indexing and increase SEO juice through a spread of the PageRank.

So when you see a drop in rankings just when you are busy creating new stuff and updating your site you feel like losing whatever hair your regular SEO activity has left you with. The fact is that websites drop in rank and there are a large number of external factors controlling that. But sometimes your own activities are a contributory factor. Clearly you cannot do anything about the factors you cannot control but you can, at least, minimize the chances of your own SEO work achieving the opposite result.

Let's see how:

1. Problem: Changing the content of established pages causes them to drop in rank. Pages the content of which is significantly increased (or decreased) which suddenly acquire a large number of links or to which the keyword density changes risk getting flagged up by Google as pages the identity of which has changed substantially and therefore either can no longer be trusted or else could, potentially, be a sign of spam site activity.

Solution: If you are going to substantially change the content and structure of high ranking pages plan it so it is done gradually over a period of time.

2. The links to your website change causing a drop in PageRank. This is more likely to affect new sites rather than established ones with a long history of high-quality, one-way links. However, the wrong type of link building strategy in place is more than likely to produce exactly this kind of problem. Usually, the reason the number of links to your site drops is because you have purchased links which have now expired, you have used links from spam sites (which are now discounted) or you have used links from sites which Google has now penalized either because they are active in an indiscriminate linking strategy or because they are selling links.

Solution: Spend time developing your links in a slow, steady way that produces high-quality links that really last and give you powerful SEO juice.

**3. Your website drops in the organic
search engine results page though you
have done nothing to upset its content or
structure**. Bear in mind the web is dynamic. It
never stands still and other webmasters are
constantly optimizing their sites for better
inclusion and deeper indexing. If you stand still
you will most likely be overtaken.

Solution: Make sure you really stick to
your daily SEO routine and broader SEO
strategy religiously. Analyze your competitors'
pages   using:
http://www.widexl.com/remote/search-
engines/metatag-analyzer.html   understand
exactly what it is they are doing and then work
not just to emulate them but actually surpass
them, producing pages that are trusted more
and are more relevant to the targeted search
queries.

**4. Your website was ranked high and
has now virtually disappeared from
Google's organic search results page
(SERPs).** If this happens you may have been
using a Black Hat SEO technique which has
been spotted. Doorway pages, hidden text,
cloaking scripts and keyword stuffing are all
techniques which will see your website being
severely penalized.

Solution: If you are reading this I'd like to
think that you are unlikely to resort to Black
Hat. If you are not sure however if what you are
doing is kosher as far as Google and the other
search engines are concerned check out Google's

SEO guidelines for webmasters: http://www.google.com/support/webmasters/bin/answer.py?answer=35769.

5. Your site's position in the organic search engine results page (SERPs) begins to fluctuate wildly, disappearing, appearing and dropping. This is a clear indication of a change in the search engine algorithm. Google tweaks its algorithm every month and carries out a significant change at least twice a year. Make sure you follow our SEO News in order to understand what these changes mean and how they affect webmasters and what you can do to make sure their impact on your site is minimized.

Solution: A search engine algorithm change needs to be ridden out until the update has finished and then the optimization process will have to begin again taking into account, this time, what's new in the search engine algorithm.

6. Server problems, uptime and 404s. If your server uptime is not good then there is a chance that your website will be down when a search engine bot tries to crawl it, which means it cannot possibly serve high pages which it has recorded in its database as being unable to find. It is important, for this reason, to check out your website's log files for 404s (page not found) messages and determine their frequency and identity. A lot of 404s will start to affect your organic search engine results (SERPs) page and your PageRank.

Solution: Make it part of your SEO routine tasks to check your website's weekly uptime log files and 404 record. Sometimes just moving hosting to a more stable server is enough to increase traffic, PageRank and organic search engine results positioning.

Summary

There are many factors which affect how you are perceived by search engines, where your site is positioned and what your PageRank is. Make sure you work on the ones you can directly control.

Action Plan

Work through each of the reasons for affecting your website's PageRank and SEO status, listed above, internalise them and then work to incorporate the proposed solution in your regular SEO activities.

13. How to use your Blog to attract search engine attention and more traffic

If you have a website you are serious about having perform well in the organic search engine results page then the heavy artillery in your arsenal will be your humble Blog.

Given the speed at which web trends develop a Blog may seem a little bit old-fashioned, particularly when you consider that sites today go for video logs (called Vlogs) and Podcasts but it is still a potent weapon which can help your site appear high on the search engine charts and, more importantly, give you a handy means of using targeted keywords in a meaningful context to profile your site.

So how is it done? I will show you here:

A Blog is a powerful tool exactly because it breaks free of the constrains of the more rigid article and the conventions that govern it and allows you to write in a freer spirit that can, often, capture the essence of what makes successful link-bait.

More than that however a Blog allows you to use very targeted keywords in a much more specific way than you would in an article and has the ability to help in the cross-linking strategy of your website which will lead to deeper indexing of your site's pages, greater accessibility and impact of your keywords and more organic search engine exposure which means more traffic.

It also has the ability to start creating a 'Voice' for your website, which allows you to get your personality across to your potential audience.

So how do you use it exactly?

The best way is to show examples. Let's take the SEO field, for instance, which is really crowded. In order for my website to show up across many relevant keywords I use the Blog as part of my ongoing optimisation effort.

One post, for instance, may be about link-bait, where I explain what it is and why you should consider it and when and then link to the section on my SEO articles which actually detail what you should do in order to create link bait on your site.

The fact that we are highlighting it on our Blog plus the cross linking plus the fact that these keywords already exist creates a powerful search engine reinforcement that promotes my website for those search terms.

The beauty of it is that in the Blog I only really need to mention things in a casual, off-hand way rather than create structured content like I have to when I write articles. Blog content can take the form of thoughts, ideas, notes and it can be as little as a paragraph and still prove effective. Even better it is perfect in terms of adding relevant, keyword-rich content to your website on a daily basis and successful websites employ it as a weapon to attract search engine attention and add content in small snippets several times a day.

Summary

A Blog allows you to add keyword-rich, relevant content to your website every single day without having to struggle with the contents of a full article.

Action Plan

Use your Blog like an online diary. Drop in snippets, relevant paragraphs and small announcements or comments. Cross-link to relevant pages on your site to draw attention to really relevant content there. Do not be afraid to let your personality shine through.

14. How to check search engine saturation

If you're working on search engine optimising your website or even if you have hired an SEO company to do it for you, you need to know the sum effect of their efforts and that sum effect is most evident in the number of pages of your site that each of the major search engines has indexed and serves up from its database.

When you look at how many of these pages are indexed two things are really important. First the sheer number of them. These show the depth of indexing that has gone on, on your site. Then you need to know exactly where these pages are in each search engine's database. Here's how you check and why:

Let's begin from the beginning. You have a website that has 100 pages or more. If Google has only indexed ten of those pages your website is underperforming. First Google thinks it is a lot smaller than it is and therefore relatively unimportant. Secondly you are missing out on the opportunity to have as many relevant search terms as possible showing up for your website. Thirdly, if your site is not being indexed properly it may be indicative of other things which are wrong with it which are hurting its SEO standing.

By the same token if you are in the situation where you are paying out hundreds of dollars each month so that someone can optimise your website you need to know that they are doing a great job which should mean that the number of pages indexed by each search engine should be equal to the number of pages you have on your website. If they are not there should be regular, almost daily growth in that number.

This leads us to the question of how do you check. It used to be that each of the major search engines (that's Google, Yahoo! and MSN in that exact order) database needed to be queried independently in order to give results in that.

No longer. The standardisation process that has been evident in some of the aspects of search engine development now allows for the same query in all three.

Simply go to: www.google.com
www.yahoo.com
www.bing.com

and in each search window, in turn, type the following search engine query command: site:http://www.mysitename.com replacing the search term 'mysitename' with the name of your website.

The results that this will return will give you the number of pages of your website that have been indexed in each one.

Perform this action on a daily basis. If you see the number of pages dropping it is a sign that your website is having SEO issues and the search engines are dropping pages from their main index.

The other thing you need to check is where exactly in the Google database your site's pages appear. If you are not sure how to find pages which are less deeply indexed or not as regularly refreshed in the Google database go to: http://www.google.com/webmasters/ and sign up for Google's FREE Webmaster Tools service. This will give you the kind of information you need for your website which will help you fine-tune your optimization efforts through fresher content on those troubled pages, a deeper linking strategy, more cross-linking or simply bringing pages which may be buried deeper in your site's structure (like older articles for example) to the surface through a Blog Archive or similar feature.

Summary

You need to check regularly on the major search engines to see just how many pages of your website have been indexed and are in their database. The results you will get by querying each search engine are a clear indication of your website's SEO health.

Action Plan

Follow the steps above and find out how many of your website's pages are listed in each search engine. Make a note of the date of your check and the results and compare it every two-three days to make sure you spot if there is any negative influence.

15. SEO Toolbars

When you have a website you want to optimize
and market to search engines time is always
against you. You are always struggling to find
ways to automate some processes so that you
can free up the time necessary to make
valuable business decisions.

In practical terms this means that you are
always on the lookout for tricks of the trade
which will help you both in your analysis of
websites and some of the SEO activities you
need in order to promote your website to search
engines and online visitors.

The fact that, in this respect at least, we
are all in the same boat means that some
solutions have been found.

The most potent of these are in the SEO
tools incorporated in the toolbar of the Firefox
browser. So let's go and see how you can get
these and how you can use them.

Step 1 - Firefox

Get the Firefox browser (if you haven't already).
For a quick (very quick) knowledge lesson,
Mozilla Firefox is a free and open source web
browser descended from the Mozilla Application
Suite and managed by the Mozilla Corporation.
A Net Applications survey put Firefox at 25% of
the recorded usage share of web browsers as of

November 2009, making it the second most popular browser in terms of current use worldwide after Microsoft's Internet Explorer, and the most used browser independent of any one operating system.

To display web pages, Firefox uses the Gecko layout engine, which implements most current web standards in addition to several features which are intended to anticipate likely additions to the standards.

The latest Firefox features include tabbed browsing, spell checking, incremental find, live bookmarking, a download manager, private browsing, location-aware browsing (aka "geolocation") based exclusively on a Google service and an integrated search system that uses Google by default in most localizations.

Firefox runs on various versions of Mac OS X, Microsoft Windows, Linux, and many other Unix-like operating systems.

At the time of writing it has an annoying instability which makes it make inefficient usage of the CPU and overheat (not good if you are running it on a netbook or mini-PC, so don't) and sometimes it also, for no apparent reason, cuts out and closes down.

Browser technology is still in evolution so, these two known bugs aside, it is a fairly stable browser and about as useful as they come.

Firefox can be downloaded free from: http://www.mozilla.com/en-US/firefox/firefox.html so, if you have not already installed it in your system point your

browser there and download it now. You are
going to need it.

If you happen to have it already, fire it up,
make sure it is the latest version and let's go
and see how we can use it to help make your
SEO life easier.

Step 2 – Add SEOquake

Once you have your Firefox browser all lit up
put in the address window the following
destination: http://www.seoquake.com/

SEOquake is a useful SEO tool which
integrates in the Firefox browser. Download it
and install it.

SEOquake allows you to analyze some very
useful search engine optimization parameters
of sites you visit at the click of a button.

The elements you analyze include: keyword
saturation, the number of pages of the site you
are visiting in the Google, Yahoo! and BING
search engine databases, the number of pages
linking to the site you are visiting and the
number of backlinks which have been indexed
by each search engine.

The application queries Alexa as well as all
of the major search engines (you can see a
demonstration of its versatility when it comes
to research in this YouTube video:
http://www.youtube.com/watch?v=NvYWBYpR
GHY).

SEOquake is a powerful SEO analysis tool
in your own pages as well as those of

competitors for specific keywords and search terms. One word of advice, make sure you have SEOquake switched off when you are browsing and then switch it on only when you need to analyze a particular website.

This way you prevent being banned by the Google search engine for taking up too many of its resources with constant queries.

Step 3 – Add KGen for keyword analysis

KGen (Keyword Generator) is a Firefox extension that allows you to see what keywords are strong on a visited web page. Then you can retrieve those keywords and use them for social sharing (tag filling) or web mastering / SEO purpose.

Its main strength however comes in helping you analyze quickly the competitive keywords a competing website employs so you can emulate them or counter them through your own online campaign.

KGen does not replace your own in-depth analysis of a website but it is great when speed rather than depth is what counts.

To download KGen point your Firefox browser to and add it to your Firefox add ons: https://addons.mozilla.org/en-US/firefox/addon/4788.

Once it has been installed, place your cursor on the FireFox toolbar and click on 'Customize'. Then find the KGen icon in the

dialogue box which opens up and drag it and
drop it into the FireFox toolbar.

This will add KGen to your active FireFox
tools. When you are on a website you need to
analyze quickly a click on KGen opens up a side
tab on your browser which enables you to see
keywords, arrange them by importance, see
them in a tag cloud, see tags, export them, and
see what it is that makes a particular page
work so well in terms of the keywords it has on
it.

Step 4 – Add ADDThis to your Firefox toolbar

This is the final SEO tool you need to add to our
Firefox browser and it will greatly complement
what you already have there plus it will save
you heaps of time when it comes to publicizing
a particular website.

I will explain why you need AddThis and
how to use it in a minute, but right now let's
just go and get it.

Point your FireFox browser to:
http://www.addthis.com/. When you are there
go to the bottom right hand side of the page and
click on the Download link you will find there to
add this to your Firefox.

Once you have added it go through the
same procedure I outlined above in order to add
this to the FireFox toolbar. When you have it
your FireFox Toolbar will have a Red Cross-like

button on it which when you click on it gives you a drop down list with some of the major social tagging websites available right now.

In Chapter Five of this book we saw that social tagging sites help spread the word about your site, give you relevant traffic and help you get indexed faster.

The AddThis button helps you social tag your website's content right from your Firefox toolbar in a lot less time than if you were doing it regularly one social tag website at a time.

By remembering the login and password to the social tag sites and by automatically pre-filling the data fields required in keywords, title and descriptions you can use Firefox to automate some of the vital SEO and online publicity tasks which should be part of the routine required to make your that your online presence is strong, vibrant and up to date.

Step 5 - Fine-tune your website's content

I have talked about the importance of keywords before. As a matter of fact, when you strip SEO activity from much of the technical stuff you have to do what remains is content and keywords. Simple, right?

That's where many go wrong. Very wrong. The temptation, for example, to optimize a website straight off, for the name of the product it sells is so great that very few webmasters can resist it. Broadly speaking that is not a bad thing to do, but bearing in mind that time is money and creating content, waiting to be indexed and then waiting for an appraisal of the results in terms of traffic numbers and purchases made (which, after all is the clearest indication of the SEO success of your website and its ability to attract targeted visitors) all take time, by the time you have got to the point that you begin to realize that something is wrong with your SEO efforts you have spent a heck of a lot of money.

So, let's get straight to the point: What should you be doing, right from the start, in order to make sure your SEO efforts are bang on what they should be?

The trick here is in wearing the right hat when you approach SEO. When you are creating your list of keywords which will guide your content creation and website optimization efforts, do not just approach the project from the expert, owner, with in-depth product knowledge angle, but look at your site and the way it sells its products and services, from a purely customer or first-time visitor angle.

Here is an example which drives the point home: When we first launched HelpMySEO, within four days it made Google's top page for the search term 'Help My SEO' against over 14 million competing pages at the time. Had we been planning to optimize it for that search term (we had not) we would have been justified in popping champagne corks and getting the catering people to throw a small party for us.

That would have been incredibly short-sighted. For a start, 'Help My SEO' is a term which we would assume (quite correctly) that few people looking for SEO tips or SEO help for their site would actually type in a search engine. Even worse, for a new webmaster, the term 'Help My SEO' is about as outlandish as typing 'newly-minted webmaster independently seeks on-page optimization tips for nascent website', which, I hope, perfectly illustrates the problem.

In order to be successful we had to approach the search terms that would be typed in a search engine from a new-user point of view, looking for tips and advice on how to optimize their website.

This is exactly what you should be doing for your website when creating your list of keywords. You need to think if you were completely new, knew nothing about the business and were looking for a product or service your website sells, what would you type in the search engine, hoping to find it?

Sometimes, it's lucky and the search terms which come up exactly describe the product or service you happen to sell through your website. But, in more cases than you would think, the search terms entered by users are not the same as the search terms you have been optimizing your website for and there, exactly, lies the problem.

So, make sure the list of keywords you are using is truly user-orientated in the way you generate them, rather than webmaster-generated (which is usually the case). Use pen and paper, write down the pertinent questions from a user's point of view and think of the keywords they are most likely to be using when looking for your website and then make sure you have optimized content for those keywords.

This will save you time and money and, most important of all, it will drive highly targeted visitors to your site.

16. Dance with Google

Whether you like it or not two facts are true in the online world: 1. Google is part of everyday online life and 2. You cannot do anything to control Google.

When your success and online survival depends on something so totally outside your control your survival strategy revolves around your ability to understand it and detect changes in it before they become too apparent.

Google Dance is a free tool which allows you to query specific Google databases and see how each treats a particular website (or websites).

There are many reasons why this is good SEO. First, Google rolls out and tests changes in its algorithm in datacenters which serve fewer queries and have smaller databases. This can be its Australian base (for English), or its French or Greek datacenter.

By checking once or twice a month how your website is faring in these centers you are placing yourself in the best position possible to detect changes in the Google algorithm before they are rolled out in the major datacenters and then, take the steps necessary to make your site adapt for them and perform better.

Google Dance can be found here: http://www.seochat.com/googledance/

Meta Description counts for Google

Improve your website's SEO status with Google almost immediately by rewriting its meta description

The meta tags of your site still count in terms of the importance given to them by search engines. Because of abuse however they are no longer take purely at their word. Google has a number of strategies for selecting snippets and the meta name description of your website is one of them.

As a webmaster trying to optimize your site you cannot control Google's indexing strategies but you can control the meta tags on your website and making sure that the meta description is optimized can help you a great deal.

Before we go any further let's get straight the fact that a really well optimized meta description will not affect the organic search engine page result of your website nor will it affect its PageRank. What it will affect however is the way surfers read it on the organic search engine results page and how many of them then decide to click upon it. Simply put, if you optimize your meta description tag so that it reads properly, more of those who find it will click on it, visit your site and access your services or buy your products.

Ideally, in a dynamic website, you should be writing an individual meta description tag for each page.

In your site's code the meta description tag looks like this:

<META   NAME="Description" CONTENT="informative description here">

This is what Google have on their own site regarding meta descriptions:

"Why does Google care about meta descriptions?

We want snippets to accurately represent the web result. We frequently prefer to display meta descriptions of pages (when available) because it gives users a clear idea of the URL's content. This directs them to good results faster and reduces the click-and-backtrack behavior that frustrates visitors and inflates web traffic metrics. Keep in mind that meta descriptions comprised of long strings of keywords don't achieve this goal and are less likely to be displayed in place of a regular, non-meta description, snippet. And it's worth noting that while accurate meta descriptions can improve clickthrough, they won't affect your ranking within search results."

For instructions on how to change your website's title and description which Google indexes   check   out:
http://www.google.com/support/webmasters/bin/answer.py?hl=en&answer=35264

Get your description meta tag content right and you should see an increase in targeted traffic to you site almost immediately.

17. Facebook marketing

With over 200 million global users Facebook has emerged as one of the social networking success stories of our times. It has also become a potent marketing tool which can help increase sales, traffic and the SEO status of your website. Provided, of course, you understand exactly what you need to do in order to achieve the desired results.

In this chapter I will tell you what you need to do and why in order to successfully use Facebook to market your website.

First of all let's examine what the result of a successful SEM campaign will be in Facebook. First you will get a lot of traffic. Second you may convert some of that traffic into sales. Third some of that Facebook traffic may pass on details about your site to others in their network thereby becoming for you vital viral marketing aids, do remember that the interaction of Facebook members with your postings is visible to their own networks of friends and contacts which may then be tempted to follow the links themselves.

Even if two and three do not happen, the very fact that you have direct, real traffic coming to your website will begin to affect the way Google sees your site which will begin to rise in terms of organic status. This will lead to a rise in the SERPs and more natural, targeted traffic, a case of success breeding success.

Converting that success to sales will then be your job.

Ok, theory lesson over, let's go and look at the practice.

First of all you need to go to Facebook (www.facebook.com) and create an account if you do not have one already. Depending on how you are going to promote your website you will need to think of the type of account profile you will have. For instance: some website owners find it easier to create a fictitious woman with a semi-provocative image or a very pretty head and shoulders picture and use that to send invitations to a lot of Facebook males.

Others find it is more expedient to create a more generic listing and then look at all the networks that may be interested (example is a network on Fashion if you are selling shoes or clothes or make up). Or a regional network (like, for instance LA) if you are selling locally or have a strong local presence. This then becomes a powerful way to market locally leveraging the cost-effectiveness of the web and its accessibility.

You need to remember that Facebook is a social network and even if you decide that a corporate presence is what you need, you still need to interact with a 'human face' and have a persona which represents your organization.

Once you have decided on the profile you need to create you will need to decide how exactly you will approach Facebook users in order to entice them to your website. A simple: "Good products or services sold here, visit this site" is not going to work.

Think in terms of a clever message and a strong, original content page with links to different products or services. One of our clients who has a site that delivers original content to students seeking essays for their term papers created an entire page on his site debating whether getting a term paper written up is cheating or not. He then looked up all the groups which had the terms 'Study and Studying' using Facebook's search facility and he became a member of each through his profile.

Once he had all the groups in place he proceeded to post a topic about what exactly is cheating in today's world on the topic board of each group with a link heading back to the page he had created on his website. On that page, at the bottom, he also made sure that students could click and order an essay if they wanted to.

The result? Within three days of creating this campaign he had reached a student population more than 1 million strong. Visits to his website rose from 50 per day to over 300 and this traffic remained steady for more than two weeks before dropping again to about 60 – 70 per day.

The increased attention made his site move up on Google's organic results page by four places in just two weeks. What's more it remained at that position even after the traffic dropped to the previous level.

More important he had achieved brand awareness in a highly targeted audience and in just two weeks had achieved sales worth $20,000.

Now he has made Facebook marketing part of his natural online campaign routine. He is careful not to overdo it. He targets selective groups and he times it so that it hits them when they at their most receptive.

This real-life case study gives you the recipe you need for Facebook marketing success: 1. Be original 2. Be timely 3. Be relevant (do not spam groups by posting an invitation for shoes in a Book Discussion group, for example). 4. Make the campaign a regular event and fine tune it after you have the results of the first one. 5. Try to expand your marketing by thinking what other networks or groups on Facebook you can approach.

18. The marketing power of Twitter

Twitter is an oddity in the online marketing toolbox. It is a microblogging site with the ability to attract thousands of followers and it is undeniably possessed of a certain addictive quality which its adherent swear by.

As I write all this there are large corporations with marketing departments staffed by PR experts and professional journalists who are still struggling to find ways to use Twitter meaningfully.

The best way here is to first understand what Twitter is not.

1. Twitter is not a platform for blatantly blasting product after product and service after service. Its 140-character restriction strips it of any such potential and only makes it work against you.

2. Twitter is not the kind of marketing you start and stop or only use if all you are after some quick publicity.

3. Twitter is not of any use if what it gives does not contain some inherent value.

So what is it that makes Twitter so hot in terms of online marketing? Just like Facebook. Twitter's potential lies in the fact that it has now become one of the hottest new online hangouts to mingle and socialize on the web. As such Twitter enjoys immense marketing possibilities out of a sheer magnitude of users, all swarming in one spot ready to lap up and spread interesting, unique and usable messages.

If you have not yet got a Twitter account (and Twitter is one of the social tagging sites which appear in the social marketing tools which, just three chapters ago, I suggested you add to the Firefox toolbar) then go to www.twitter.com and create one. Twitter gives you the ability to customize it like this: http://twitter.com/DavidAmerland creating a more professional appearance.

How to become a successful Twitter user

Here are some steps you can follow to become a successful online marketer on Twitter.

1. The first step is to create a Twitter account, this is fairly easy process, and you will end up with an account for your marketing campaign at twitter like this: http://twitter.com/DavidAmerland. Remember, if you are going to promote a particular product it is then best to create separate accounts whose names are related to the product/service you are going to promote. This should happen even if you have a personal Twitter account. This will look more professional in the long run

to have a dedicated following comprised exclusively of the target audience and it will allow you to keep your personal account for your more quirky personal tweets (i.e., individual posts to Twitter).

2. Customize the profile. Once the account has been created, tweak the profile details to make it attractive to the target audience. Add an original logo, match the color of the profile with that of the logo, include keywords about the product/service to be promoted, add pictures and bits of information which are interesting and usable and fill in all the sidebar information.

3. Put badges on your website. Twitter allows your audience to know when you have posted something they are interested in, even if they are not on your site, or on Twitter or even online. Putting badges on your website and the web pages related to your promotion will allow your online visitors to follow you on Twitter.

4. Seek followers. This is the most important aspect of Twitter, whether you are doing it for personal reasons or for a marketing advantage. Web marketers seek quality followers from the business vertical in which they are promoting their product or service. This can be done by going through the profiles and tweets posted by various followers and getting noticed by contributing to their conversations

5. Jump in and reply to interesting @-reply tweets, which are public conversations between two users. Check out both parties and

"follow" them if they interest you. If you follow someone with, say, 10,000 followers and reply to his/her posts meaningfully for long enough, chances are good that he/she will start to reply to you and start following you.

6. Retweet. Retweeting means forwarding someone else's tweet to your own follower list. Proper retweeting can go a long way in gaining invaluable followers who are very popular themselves. Credit your Tweet source by adding their @ tag; e.g., when DavidAmerland, whom you follow, sends out, "Great new SEO tip at http://helpmyseo.com" retweet it to your list as "RT @DavidAmerland: Great new SEO tip at http://helpmyseo.com." If you have characters to spare, you can spell out ReTweet. If someone with 10,000 followers retweets your posts, their followers may retweet your post and so on, with the potential for massive exposure.

Things to remember as you build your twitter campaign

1. Create buzz. The moment you have got a sizable number of people following you and you have the power of replying and retweeting and you want to write a new post to appear on your website. But before actually writing the post, start creating a buzz through tweets.

2. Tweet your post. You have the retweet power, and you have created the buildup. It is time to tweet your post. So do it, make sure

that it brings some value to your followers. Don't be repetitive or boring.

3. Tweet constant reminders. This is an important part of successful tweeting. Keep posting reminder tweets which are different from one another and lead to different aspects of the post. You should also time your reminders by gauging when the most of your followers are also posting, which indicates that they're also reading their own messages.

Twitter Success Tips

* Be Useful. Create value for your readers.

* Be Timely. Post when the most of your followers are online.

* Be Willing to Engage. Don't create impersonal and vague tweets as if you're in an isolated bubble; rather, interact with the reader and with the world. Reply to individuals and join the public conversation.

Twitter Warnings to be aware of

* Don't be a spammer. People do not want direct messaging to be used for promotion.

* You will gain followers if you post interesting tweets on a number of diverse topics and if you give credit to others when you retweet.

19. SEO or PPC and how to decide

The moment you start talking SEO and PPC you land squarely into Google's lap. The search engine's dominance in organic search engine page results means that the moment you start spending money to search engine optimize your site you are forced to look very carefully at a number of factors such as visitor numbers (which means traffic volumes), the conversion ratio of those visitors (which will help you determine, in part, the Return on your Investment or ROI) and the quality of the customers you get.

You will also want to run the same analysis on your pay-per-click (PPC) campaign otherwise you cannot have a meaningful, like for like comparison between the two. Provided you are ready to pull money from PPC and focus it on SEO what should you expect?

While every site is unique and every site's profile on the net is unique we shall assume for the purposes of this exercise that your site is superbly search engine optimized and that you have decent search engine marketing in place which has began to provide you with results in terms of traffic. So the question is what should the SEO vs PPC picture be like?

Experience with sites I have worked with shows that on average you should expect the organic search engine traffic to outweigh your PPC traffic by at least twenty to one. Which means you should be getting twenty organic search provided visitors for every one your pay-per-click campaign gives you.

So far this is ok and it shows the value of having a highly search engine optimized and search engine marketed website. The next question, however, which deals with conversion rates on your online visitors is much harder to answer and the reason is because it depends on the focus of your PPC and the focus of your SEO.

If, for instance, your PPC campaign is really tightly focused in terms of the keywords you have chosen then the return you will have from that will be far better than anything your organic campaign is giving you. Similarly if your SEO is really tightly focused with keywords which are very relevant to your content and the nature of your online business then the conversion ratio of your SEO will be higher than average.

If, for argument's sake, we assume that your website is optimized for the usual 200 - 250 keywords most websites are optimized for these days, which means you spread the organic campaign to bring in as much traffic as possible, then the conversion ration of your PPC will be much higher.

The exception to this rule are sites which have a sufficiently broad appeal to work well

from a large natural SEO catchment and these
are, traditionally, online advertising sites,
artists-studios, online real estate sites and
community sites.

Finally you will want to look at the quality
and value of each online customer you convert.
This is a very important consideration because
it gives you a true picture of what you spend in
order to gain one customer and what you obtain
in return.

You may find this online calculator which
helps you gauge the return on your investment
(ROI) for a pay-per-click campaign (PPC) useful
in terms of how you control your budget:
http://www.stepmiles.com/ROI-Calculator.htm.

Traditionally sites which have a higher
organic ranking find that the customer lifetime
value is higher for organic SEO than it is for
PPC. This, depends, very much, upon the
nature of the customers. In the web savvy age,
customers respect a high organic ranking much
more than they respect a PPC campaign which
can be launched by practically anyone and this
is reflected in their willingness to do business
with the website they have found this way.

While both PPC and SEO need to be highly
targeted results from many established
websites suggest that the cost required to
target PPC precisely does not allow for a broad
enough campaign and though very tight
targeting in terms of keywords leads to a good
conversion ratio it does not lead to a healthy

enough volume of traffic, whereas natural SEO does.

Broadening a PPC campaign to achieve the same effect you could do with natural SEO is about the most wasteful thing you can do with your money. SEO delivers traffic which does not convert immediately. Because the site ranks high it allows visitors to check and come back and the conversion ratio, overall, is far more cost-effective. If you are paying for each word (as in a broad band of keywords in a PPC campaign) you may well end up with the same traffic figures but as each customer has cost you more to get the increase in conversion ratio is negligible while the increase in PPC costs is, usually, significant.

20. Alexa Rankings and how to improve them

The budding webmaster trying to SEO his website and improve his Google PageRank has enough to think about without stumbling around trying to determine whether Alexa Rankings are also something he should be fighting for.

Alexa is an Amazon.com company that purports to rank websites according to their reach, popularity and traffic and, as a result, is widely used by the online ad industry in order to determine whether the amount of money asked by a webmaster for their online advertising is really worth it.

Here is the catch: Alexa determines a website's ranking through the information it receives from those who use it and those who use it tell Alexa about it only if they have downloaded the Alexa toolbar on their web browser which means that the picture Alexa paints is inaccurate anyway.

Most people who have the Alexa toolbar on their web browser tend to be technically minded web masters rather than ordinary web surfers but that is irrelevant if one of your website's methods of monetization is getting paid advertising. The question here then is can you do anything at all to improve your website's Alexa Ranking and the answer is, thankfully, yes.

Ok, let's take things from the beginning and throw in a couple of explanations. Alexa ranks websites based on impressions sent back to it through its toolbar and through clicks sent to it through its widget (we'll explain both in just a few minutes). This means that if you can increase both of these your Alexa ranking will automatically improve.

The second ting you need to bear in mind is that it is always easy to dramatically improve the Alexa Ranking of a website that is doing very poorly than to achieve a huge increase for one which is doing ok anyway.

Now for the tactics:

1. Download and install the Alexa Toolbar http://www.alexa.com/site/download/ on your browser if you are using IE or download the Search Status extension if you are using Firefox http://www.quirk.biz/searchstatus/. Make sure that your homepage is set to start always on your website in IE you can do this through Tools>Internet Options>General. Every time you visit your site, or fire up your browser you send a hit to Alexa which counts it in its cumulative stats concerning your website.

2. Tell all your employees, family and friends to do the same.

3. Install an Alexa Widget http://www.alexa.com/site/site_stats/signup on your website. This will have an immediate effect as site visitors tend to click on it and each click actually counts towards your Alexa ranking.

The cumulative effect of these three activities is that within days you will see your Alexa website ranking improve by at least 20%.

Summary

Alexa Rankings are used by the online advertising industry as a means of gauging a website's worth in terms of paid advertising.

Action Plan

Follow each of the three steps above and make sure you have a daily routine of visiting your website each day.

Famous last words

Every book has a section where the author lists things or opinions which do not comfortably sit in the main body.

Here are mine: Throughout this book I have given you not just advice but insights which are part of the practices my colleagues and I employ to drive sites to Google's #1 page.

I know these work. I have also, throughout this book, struck a note of solid confidence. That bit is a front. In the SEO world everything is built on sand resting upon a house of cards.

A new challenge by an upstart college kid to one of the established search engines can lead to dramatic changes as a result of their response which can totally wreck the finely-tuned SEO campaign you spent months putting in place.

I have lost track of the number of times my Blackberry has buzzed at 2.00am as an irate client checked a keyword his site was being optimized for and suddenly found it dropped to page 20 of Google, spoiling his day and my sleep.

I have also lost track of the number of times I have had to rework SEO campaigns because of a Google update or a Yahoo! /BING repositioning or because my carefully laid out test websites gave me some contrary results when tested against some of Google's data centers indicating that things were once again moving in the SEO world.

Yet, despite all this, I love the online world and take its fluidity as part of online life. The steps I have given you here as part of your search engine optimization induction are unlikely to change in terms of importance for some time to come.

Since you will be working on your own website or websites you are unlikely to be woken up by irate clients who do not understand the fluidity of SEO work. You are though likely to lose sleep over it as your sites fail to perform as well as you need them to.

With this in mind I will say that the best friend any search engine optimiser can ever have is a good quality, reliable espresso machine. A hot cup of good coffee has the ability to transform any time of the day or night into your moment.

SEO Terminology

The words or phrases used by people when performing searches in search engines. Also called keywords, query terms or query.

Ad Rank - Google AdWords multiplies Quality Score (QS) and the maximum CPC (Max CPC) to reach an Ad Rank for each ad.

AdSense Arbitrage - The process of buying traffic with pay-per-click programs, sending traffic to highly optimized Adsense pages and collecting the difference.

AdSense Link Clicking Bots - Automated programs that try to spoof random IP addresses to click through AdWords displayed on a site.

Adwords - Google's - Cost Per Click (CPC) based advertising system.

ALT Text - The text that appears when you put your mouse on top of an image or a picture.

Anchor Text - Also known as Link Text, the clickable text of a hyperlink.

API - Application Programming Interface.

Authority Site - A site that has many In-Bound links coming to it, and very few outbound links.

Back link - A text link to your website from another website.

Banned - A term that means a site has been removed from a search engine's index.

Black Hat SEO - A term referring to the practice of "unethical" SEO. These techniques are used to gain an advantage over your competition.

Blog - A "Web Log" that is updated frequently and is usually the opinion of one person. Also joking stands for Better Listing on Google.

Bot - Short for robot. Often used to refer to a search engine spider.

Browser - Software application used to browse the internet - Mozilla Firefox and Internet Explorer are the 2 most popular browsers.

BTF (Below the Fold) - This is the part of the user's screen that is hidden unless the user scrolls down on the page.

C Class IP - This is the third block of numbers found in an IP Address.

Cache - A copy of web pages stored within a search engine's database.

CAPTCHA - Stands for : Completely Automated Public Turing test to tell Computers and Humans Apart.

Click Arbitrage - Purchasing PPC ads and hoping that traffic leaves with a click on your ads.

Click Distance - The minimum number of clicks it takes a visitor to get from one page to another.

Click Flipping - The process of identifying and maximizing, multiple profit pathways, using PPC traffic and converting that traffic with Cost Per Action offers.

Click Through - The process of clicking through an online advertisement to the advertiser's destination.

Clickprint - Derived from the amount of time a user spends on a Web site and the number of pages viewed, a clickprint is a unique online fingerprint that can help a vendor identify return visitors, curb fraud, and collect personal information for "customer service." aka invasive marketing.

Cloaking - A technique that shows keyword stuffed pages to a search engine, but a real page to a human user.

Clustering - In search engine search results pages, clustering is limiting each represented website to one or two listings.

Content Networks - A nicer way to say Link Farm, a Black Hat SEO technique and a Google red flag technique.

Content Repurposing - A nicer way to say scraping a site for content. It will get your site banned.

Contextual Link Inventory (CLI) - Text links that are shown depending on the content that appears around them.

Conversion Optimization - Transforms your site into a selling tool - your site logically leads visitors through the sales cycle and closes sale.

Conversion Rate - The number of visitors to a website that end up performing a specific action that leads to a conversion. This could be a product purchase, newsletter sign up or anything where information is submitted.

Converting Search Phrase - A phrase that converts traffic into money.

Cookie - Information stored on a user's computer by a website.

Cost per Thousand (CPT) - The cost for each thousand impressions of your ad.

CPA - (Cost Per Action) - The price paid for each visitor's actions from a paid search.

CPC (Cost Per Click) - The amount it will cost each time a user selects your phrase or keyword.

Crawler - A bot from a search engine that reads the text found on a website in order to determine what the website is about.

Cross Linking - Having multiple websites linking to each other.

CSS (Cascading Style Sheets) - Used to define the look and navigation of a website.

CTR (Click Through Rate) - The value associated to the amount of times a paid ad is viewed.

Dangling Link - This term is applied to a web page with no links to any other pages. Also known as an Orphan Page.

Dead Link - A hyperlink pointing to a non-existent URL.

Deep Crawl - Once a month, Googlebot will crawl all of the links it has listed in its database on your site. This is known as the Deep Crawl.

Deep Link - A link on a website that is not reachable from the home page.

Delisting - When a site gets removed from the search index of a search engine.

Diggbait - Purposely creating content to get traffic from digg.com

Directory - Usually human edited, a directory contains sites that are sorted by categories.

DMOZ - Also known as the Open Directory Project.

DNS (Domain Name System) - A protocol that lets computers recognize each other through an IP Address, whereas the human sees a website URL.

Doorway Page - A web page designed to draw in Internet traffic from search engines, and then direct this traffic to another website.

Dynamic Site - A site that uses a database to store its content and is delivered based on the variable passed to the page.

EPC (Earnings Per Click) - How much profit is **made from each click from a paid ad.**

EPV (Earnings Per Visitor) - The cost it takes to make profit from a site's total number of visitors.

Error 404 - When a hyperlink is pointing to a location on the web that doesn't exist, it is called a 404 error.

Everflux - A term associated with the constant updating of Google's algorithm between the major updates.

External Link - A link that points to another website.

FFA (Free For All) - A site where anyone can list their link. Don't waste any time submitting your site to these places.

Filter Words - Words such as is, am, were, was, the, for, do, ETC, that search engines deem irrelevant for indexing purposes. Also known as Stop words.

Flog - A fake blog, a website pretending to be a blog but actually the creation of public relations firms, the mainstream media, or professional political operatives.

Fresh Crawl - Utilizes FreshBot to review already indexed pages and any pages where the content has been updated.

FreshBot - A sister to GoogleBot, this spider crawls highly ranked sites on a very frequent basis.

Geo Targeting - Geo-targeting lets you target your Google ads to specific countries and languages. When you create a new AdWords campaign, you select the countries or regions and the language(s) for your ad. That campaign's ads will appear only to users who live in the those areas and who have selected one of those languages as their preference.

GFNR - Google First Name Rank.

Google AdWords - Google's PPC program.

Google Bombing - A technique where using the same text anchor links, many people link to a certain page, usually of irrelevant content. It has now been largely been discounted by subsequent Google algorithm upgrades.

GoogleBot - The spider that performs a deep crawl of your site.

Googlebowling - To nudge a competitor from the serps.

Heading Tag - Tag that designates headlines in the text of a site.

Hidden Text - Text that can't be seen normally in a browser.

Hit - A single access request made to the server.

Htaccess - .htaccess is an Apache file that allows server configuration instructions.

Hub - A site that has many outbound links, and few sites linking back.

IBL (In-Bound Link) - A link residing on another site that points to your site.

ICRA (Internet Content Rating Association) - The Internet Content Rating Association (ICRA) is an international, non-profit organization of internet leaders working to make the internet safer for children, while respecting the rights of content providers.

Index - A term used to describe the database that holds all the web pages crawled by the search engine for each website.

Indexing Assistance - An even more advanced form of cloaking.

Information Architecture - The gathering, organizing, and presenting information to serve a purpose.

Informational Query - A query about a topic where the user expects to be provided with information on the topic.

Internal Link - A link that points to another page within the same site. Most commonly used for navigation.

Internet Traffic Optimizer (ITO) - A broader term for a person who optimizes not only for search engines but to get traffic from other sources such as blogs, RSS feeds and articles.

IP Address (Internet Protocol Address) - how data finds its way back and forth from your computer to the internet.

IP Spoofing - A method of reporting an IP address other than your own when connecting to the internet.

JS (JavaScript) - A scripting language that provides browser functionality.

Keyword Density - A ratio of the number of occurrences of a keyword or "keyword phrase" to the total number of words on a page.

Keyword Effectiveness Index (KEI) - The KEI compares the number of searches for a keyword with the number of search results to pinpoint which keywords should be the most effective for your campaign.

Keyword Phrase - A group of words that form a search query.

Keyword Stuffing - Using a keyword or "keyword phrase" excessively in a web page, perhaps in the text content or meta tags. This is a banned SEO technique.

Landing Page - Usually used in conjunction with a PPC campaign, they are call-to-action pages that prompt the user to engage the site.

Link - Also known as a hyperlink, it is the "clickable" area of text or image that allows for navigation on the Internet.

Link Bait (Linkbaiting) - The process of getting users to link to your site.

Link Farm - A site that features links in no particular order which are totally unrelated to each other. Its main purpose is to provide links rather than content.

Link Maximization - The method of getting popular sites in your industry to link to your website.

Link Partner - A website who is willing to put a link to your site from their website. Quite often link partners engage in reciprocal linking.

Link Popularity - How many sites link to your website.

Link Text - The clickable part of a hyperlink. Also known as Anchor Text or Anchor Link.

Listings - The results that a search engine returns for a particular search term.

Mashups - Commonly thought of as a way of merging two different items, or scraping more than one source.

Meta Description Tag - Hold the description of the content found on the page.

Meta Keywords Tag - Holds the keywords that are found on the page.

Meta Search Engine - A search engine that relies on the meta data found in meta tags to determine relevancy.

Meta Tag Masking - An old trick that uses CGI codes to hide the Meta tags from browsers while allowing search engines to actually see the Meta tags.

Meta Tags - Header tags that provide information about the content of a site.

Metadata - META Tags or what are officially referred to as Metadata Elements, are found within the section of your web pages.

MFA (Made For AdSense) - A term that describes websites that are created entirely for the purpose of gaming Google Adsense to make money.

MFD - Made For Digg - Similar to MFA (Made for AdSense) sites, these sites try to get traffic from digg by having entire sites full of funny images or postings.

Mirror Sites - A mirror site is a site that exactly duplicates another site.

MSN (MicroSoft Network) - Microsoft's search engine which now has been relaunched as BING (allegedely stands for BING Is Not Google).

Natural Listing - A listing that appears below the sponsored ads, also known as Organic Listings.

Navigational Query - A query that normally has only one satisfactory result.

NOFOLLOW - An attribute used in a hyperlink to instruct search engines not to follow the link. (And pass PageRank)

Off-Page Factors - Factors that alter search engine positions that occur externally from other website's. By having many links from other sites pointing to yours is an example of Off-Page Factors.

On-Page Factors - Factors that determine search engine positions that occur internally within a page of a website. This can include site copy, page titles, and navigational structure of the site.

OOP (Over Optimization Penalty) - A theory that applies if one targets only 1 keyword or phrase, and the search engines view the linking efforts to be spam.

Organic Listing - The natural results returned by a search engine.

Orphan Page - A page that has a link to it, but has no links to any other sites.

Outbound Link - A link from your site to any other site.

Page View - Anytime a user looks at any page on a website through their browser.

PageMatch - A cost-per-click advertising program that serves your site's ad on a page that contains related content.

Paid Inclusion - A submission service where you pay a fee to a search engine and the search engine guarantees that your website will be included in its index. Paid inclusion programs will also ensure that your website is indexed very fast and crawled on regular basis. It can also be used as a term to include fee based directory submission.

Pay-Per-Click Management - Strategy, Planning and Placement of targeted keywords in the paid search results.

PPC (Pay Per Click) - A technique where placements are determined by how much id bid on a particular keyword or phrase. Can become very expensive.

PR (Google's PageRank) - Google's unique system of how it tries to predict the value of a pages rank.

Rank – Ranking - The actual position of a website on a search engine results page for a certain search term or phrase.

Reciprocal Link - When two sites link to each other.

Redirects - Either server side or scripting language that tells the search engine to go to another URL automatically.

Referral Spam - Sending multiple requests to a website spoofing the header to make it look like real traffic is being sent to another site.

Referrer - A referrer is the URL of the page that the visitor came from when he entered a website.

Relevance Rank (RR) - A system in which the search engine tries to determine the theme of a site that a link is coming from

Relevancy - Term used to describe how close the content of a page is in relation to the keyword phrase used to search.

Results Page - When a user conducts a search, the page that is displayed, is called the results page. Sometimes it may be called SERPs, which stands for "search engine results page."

Rich Internet Applications (RIA) - Applications such as Ajax and Flash that provide a better user experience by delivering content in an on-demand web environment.

Robot - Often used to refer to a search engine spider.

ROC (Return on Customer) - The value each customer brings.

ROI (Return on Investment) - The cost it takes to in order to see success on your marketing investment.

RSS Feed (Rich Site Summary or Rich Site Syndication) - RSS feeds use an XML document to publish information.

Search Engine Marketing (SEM) - The practice of getting a website found on the internet

Search Engine Optimization (SEO) - The act of altering code to a website to have optimum relevance to a search engine spider.

Search Friendly Optimization (SFO) - As the term implies, this is the process of making a website search engine friendly.

Search Query - The text entered into the search box on a search engine.

SERP (Search Engine Results Page) - The results that are displayed after making a query into a search box.

SFO - Search Friendly Optimization.

Sitemap (Site Map) - A page that lists all of the critical navigation points of a website.

SPAM - Unwanted email or irrelevant content delivered. (or as some say, Site Placed Above Mine)

Spamming - The act of delivering unwanted messages to the masses.

Spider - The software that crawls your site to try and determine the content it finds.

Spiderbaiting - A technique that makes a search engine spider find your site.

Splash Page - A page displayed for viewing before reaching the main page.

Stickiness - How influential your site is in keeping a visitor on your page.

Strategic Linking - A thought out approach to getting websites to link to your site.

Submission - The process of submitting URL(s) to search engines or directories.

SWOT - A methodic way of identifying your Strengths and Weaknesses, and of examining the Opportunities and Threats you face.

Theme - What the site's main topic is about.

Title Tag - It should be used to describe the web page using targeted keywords using no more that 60 characters, including spaces.

TLD (Top Level Domain) - Most commonly thought of as a ".com", also includes ".org" and ".edu"

Tracking URL - Usually used in PPC campaigns, it is a URL that has special code added to it so that results can be monitored.

Traffic - The number of visitors a website receives over a given period. Usually reported on a monthly basis.

Transactional Query - A query where the user expects to conduct a transaction.

Trusted Feed - A form of paid inclusion which uses bulk a XML feed to directly send website content to search engines for indexing. The feed can be optimized so that your website can take advantage of better rankings and therefore more traffic.

TrustRank - A method of using a combination of limited human site review in conjunction with a search engines algorithm.

Unique Visitor - When a user visits a website, his/her IP address is logged so if he/she returns later on that day, the visit won't be counted as a unique visit but as a page impression.

Universal Search - Launched on May 16, 2007, this is Google's attempt to deliver the best result from the web. This can include video, images, news, podcasts or any other form of digital content.

URL (Uniform Resource Locator) - Commonly referred to as the domain name, this is how humans navigate through the Internet, whereas computers use IP addresses.

Web Saturation - How many pages of your site are indexed by the search engines collectively.

White Hat SEO - A term that refers to ethical practice of SEO methodologies that adhere to search engine

Other books by the same author

Books available from Mobipocket.com the Sony Bookstore, all major online eBook retailers as well as www.webdirectstudio.com and www.helpmyseo.com

Stay ahead of the competition

SEO is a fluid filed which changes rapidly. Stay ahead of your competitors and find out the latest trends, developments and techniques by subscribing to the RSS Feed of www.helpmyseo.com

The RSS Feed you need is:

http://helpmyseo.com/index.php?format=feed&type=rss

Get it Direct!

If you ever find yourself in need of a new website, some help to optimize an existing website or help with any print project check out the guys at www.webdirectstudio.com. They work hard, are easy to get along with, enjoy their work and are thoroughly professional in their approach plus I am in their debt for putting up with my eccentricities at times.

About the Author

David Amerland is a British journalist. He cut his teeth in the ELan pages of The European and joined the tide of misfits trawling the writing waves of the world when Bob Maxwell's publishing empire crumbled towards the end of the last century. He has, since, been involved in writing, publishing and web development launching a series of companies which have explored each frontier. He gained valuable experience in running corporations by being actively involved with the John Lewis Partnership between 1995 – 2002. He has used that to help guide corporations which range from leading Printing Companies in Greece to international Food Importers. He knows that all this makes him difficult to categorize while keeping him gainfully employed. He has an abiding passion for martial arts, Zen and surfing and looks for the unity of all things in everything he does. If you happen to find it before him be kind enough to let him know.

Breinigsville, PA USA
13 November 2010
249308BV00003B/2/P